C000070119

Susie Hare

A Different Song

A Different Song

The Christian songwriter's own joyous story
as she lives with Parkinson's Disease

**kevin
mayhew**

kevin
mayhew

First published in Great Britain in 2015 by Kevin Mayhew Ltd
Buxhall, Stowmarket, Suffolk IP14 3BW
Tel: +44 (0) 1449 737978 Fax: +44 (0) 1449 737834
E-mail: info@kevinmayhew.com

www.kevinmayhew.com

© Copyright 2015 Susie Hare.

The right of Susie Hare to be identified as the author of this work has been
asserted by her in accordance with the Copyright, Designs and Patents Act 1988.

The publishers wish to thank all those who have given their permission to
reproduce copyright material in this publication.

Every effort has been made to trace the owners of copyright material and
we hope that no copyright has been infringed. Pardon is sought and apology
made if the contrary be the case, and a correction will be made in any
reprint of this book.

All rights reserved. No part of this publication may be reproduced, stored in a
retrieval system, or transmitted, in any form or by any means, electronic,
mechanical, photocopying, recording, or otherwise, without the prior
written permission of the publisher.

Unless stated otherwise, Scripture quotations are taken from *The New Revised
Standard Version Bible: Anglicized Edition*, copyright 1989, 1995, Division of
Christian Education of the National Council of the Churches of Christ in the
United States of America. Used by permission. All rights reserved.

9 8 7 6 5 4 3 2 1 0

ISBN 978 1 84867 794 4
Catalogue No. 1501491

Cover design by Rob Mortonson
Edited by John Cox
Typeset by Chris Coe

Printed and bound in Great Britain

Contents

David Pawson writes   6

A word from Susie   11

The early years   13

'You must teach! You must teach!'   19

College by the sea   25

New big-innings (marrying the cricketer)   29

Mother   33

Babies, blessings and the booze ban   43

Busy, busy, busy   55

Helping to pay the school fees   63

Decision time   67

Birth of *The Bridge*   71

Parkinson's: mine for life   77

He's on my case   83

Don't forget we're C of E   89

They call me Gritty Granny   97

My heart, not my hands   101

Lyrics to songs   105

David Pawson writes

My wife and I were embarrassed, even ashamed, to discover how little we knew about Susie Hare. We had been in her delightful home once (for a charity sale) and she had visited ours once.

We had known her as the 'organist' at the church we attended and frequently commented on the life and meaning she injected into the musical part of the worship. We all missed her greatly when she had to give this up.

These warm and witty memoirs have been an eye-opener. We had no idea how great a contribution she had made to schools and churches. Of course, we were aware of the hymn book she had published and were totally sympathetic with her aim of building 'The Bridge' between the rich, devotional treasury of hymns ancient and more ancient and contemporary tunes and lyrics.

We have sung some of her compositions and consider them worthy of standing alongside those of her male counterpart, Graham Kendrick. Her poetic ability may be seen in the autobiographical rhymes which are interspersed among the fascinating and readable prose of her 'ramblings' (her word).

She pays deserved tribute to those who have influenced her: her Methodist mother, of whom John Wesley himself would have been justly proud and who well knew how to live and die for the Lord; her devoted husband and partner, Rob, who lived up to his surname in the speed with which he captured her, and is now happy to be her help-meet.

Above all, this is an extended testimony to what the Lord can do with a mischievous, self-willed, yet gifted child, which will comfort some parents. I love the asides at the close of paragraphs when she takes readers into her confidence and reveals what she really thought.

However, what shines through the whole narrative, yet is never mentioned, is the sheer courage with which she has met life head on, particularly when struck down with an incurable disease which attacked her at the very point of what she most enjoyed. I can only imagine what it must have felt to be so full of fun on the inside yet unable to show it on the outside.

It has been a joy to get to know Susie better in this way. I was surprised when she asked for a foreword, but if I can help her to get a wider readership, I shall count that a privilege.

When leukaemia took our eldest daughter at thirty-six, I had the temerity to ask the Lord for his opinion of her, only to get the unexpected reply: 'She's one of my successes.' Susie Hare is another.

A different song

I woke, as from a dream, and found
my life had crashed upon the ground
and everything was rearranged.
My life had been completely changed.

But this was not a dream, you see,
it was a stark reality
which brought to bear my greatest fear:
to lose the thing I held so dear.

For, music that I felt inside
was to the listening ear denied,
when hands, which for God's glory played,
were cruelly weakened in their praise.

It shamed me to admit it now;
without my hands I knew not how
to worship him. What could I do?
This was the only way I knew.

And then I heard the Father say,
'I do delight to hear you play,
but you, my child, must understand –
I want your heart, not just your hands.

That's what I've longed for you to give,
for then the life that you now live
will be much fuller than before:
I want to give you so much more!
Each day, your hands will stronger be
and you will play again for me.'

And so it is, that by his grace,
from a much deeper, richer place
within my heart, new songs I bring
to honour and to worship him.
The music, once again, plays on,
but now I live a different song.

A word from Susie

Having long been of the opinion that writing a book about one's life was a rather self-indulgent exercise, I was astonished when the idea popped itself into my own head and refused to budge. I was certain I wouldn't have put it there myself and I knew of only one other person who would.

The more I thought about the idea, the more I realised what a privilege it would be to share what God has done in my life through his gift of music and his abundance of grace.

It was a prompting I couldn't ignore, and so I embark on these pages, trusting that my ramblings will bear witness to God's love and faithfulness when life doesn't go quite as we expected.

The early years

On Sunday, 24 August 1947, after spending the final five months of pregnancy in bed with thrombosis, my mother gave birth to what was almost certainly the cause of it: me. My safe arrival was something of a relief, given the precarious state of Mother's health, and even my father was delighted once he'd got over the disappointment of not having a boy.

My sisters, Elinor and Maggie, then aged thirteen and eleven, had a considerable share of responsibility for the new family member whilst Mother gradually returned to good health. I remember practically nothing of my early years, but if the recollections my sisters have of them are true, it would appear that I was a stubborn little brat – which is why I think they must be false. Me, stubborn?

Also living in our house was a lady called Joy. She had come to Basingstoke to work and had asked the minister of my parents' church if he knew of anyone with whom she could stay until she sorted herself out. His first thought was us. If I was a stubborn child, then it was probably due to the confusion of having two 'mothers' plus two older sisters all telling me what to do. It was easier to take no notice of any of them.

I imagine my father felt slightly outnumbered by females but our new lodger wasn't planning to stay for more than a few weeks. She fitted in well and was a great help in our busy household, quickly forming a special bond with me in particular. It was Joy who, when I was a year old, came to get me up from my afternoon rest, to find that a pigeon had flown in the open window and was sitting at the bottom of my cot. I am told that it was not me, but she who did the screaming. Something in my subconscious must have taken root and I have been frightened of birds ever since. It was Joy who remembered me 'running fastilly' down a steep hill, unable to stop, and finally coming to a halt just inches from a car. It was Joy who played snakes and ladders with me and always let me win. It was Joy who cut the crusts off my bread when no one was looking. It was Joy who gave me parma violet sweets during the sermon at church, and it was Joy who married the man who lodged next door, by which time her intended few weeks with us had actually been nine years.

On the basis that I was already playing the piano in preference to playing with dolls, and in the belief that I should be properly taught before I established too many wrong techniques, my parents sent me to piano lessons when I was four. My teacher's first words were, 'Tell me what you know already.' I confidently announced that I knew where middle C was. It was bang opposite the keyhole; everyone knew that. 'Show me then,' she barked. I looked down at the piano, could find no keyhole and promptly burst into tears. 'So you don't really know then, do you?' she barked again. She covered my hands with a tea towel when I was playing so that I got used to the 'feel of the keyboard' without looking at it (never did know what that meant), and rapped my knuckles with a ruler when I played a wrong note. On the few occasions when she decided I deserved it, she took me down the garden to a pond and made me put my hand in the water to 'feel the fairies'. I decided, as a four-year-old does, that she was quite horrid; my parents concurred, and I left.

My relationship with Miss Reynolds had been doomed from the start, largely on account of my lack of cooperation with the tea towel routine and my staunch refusal to believe in the existence of fairies. Angels, on the other hand, were something else, and my second piano teacher was one. I adored her. She taught in various places in Hampshire and our house was the venue for her Basingstoke pupils. On every other day of the week, the piano room was a chilly place to practise in, having a kind of musty smell that pervades a room which isn't often used;

but on Wednesday afternoons the fire was lit, the flowers were arranged and the wonderful Miss Mary Brutnell was given the kind of four-star treatment as befits an angel.

My primary school years were fairly unremarkable, and my achievements were few, preferring as I did to be playing with the boys or playing the piano. My attention span was minimal (still is) and I got bored very quickly (still do). The school was very near my house and I used to wonder if there would be enough minutes to run home at playtime to see my mother. One day I risked it, thinking she would be thrilled to see me, but I was sent straight back to school with a considerable flea in my ear.

I have no recollection whatsoever of any work, although I must have done some. The only thing I recall with any clarity (and huge embarrassment) was a Christmas play. I was one of eight shepherds who did a little dance round a maypole (I know, don't ask), at the end of which we had to lift our crooks on high and shout, 'Hey!' So carried away was I with the thrill of it all, I did my 'Hey' too early and threw the whole routine into disarray.

Whilst on honeymoon, twenty years later, Rob and I were looking round Coventry Cathedral and we bumped into my teacher. 'You probably don't remember me,' I said hopefully.

'Oh yes I do,' she replied. 'You were the shepherd who hey-ed in the wrong place!' I'd rather she had remembered that I was the fastest runner in the school and represented it in the County Sports. (Difficult to imagine that now but believe me, I went like the wind.) I congratulated my teacher on her good memory and moved on before she could remember anything else that would show me up in front of my new husband.

I grew up in a house full of music. One of my sisters played the cello, the other played the violin, Dad played the organ, I played the clarinet (badly) and the violin (even more badly) and we all played the piano. I include Mother as a pianist, only on the basis of what we called her 'dusting tune'. She used to dust the piano keys with a great flourish, then play the first line of 'Crimond' (for some reason preferring it in four flats), wait for our applause, then resume the dusting. Those four bars were the only thing in her repertoire, for which we were all rather grateful.

My father had a successful business, buying, selling, repairing and (mostly) tuning pianos. Some people expected him to be blind; piano-tuners often are visually impaired and, indeed, Dad did employ one such person. Moreover, some people were surprised that he was even musical (he was, extremely). It was his custom, having completed the tuning, to check out his work with a bit of improvisation and one day, a small boy who had been watching him ran to his mother, exclaiming, 'Mummy, that piano man can play tunes as well!' Earning a living was just a necessary sideline. That piano man would have happily played tunes all day. The nearest he got to that was a Saturday job he had as a teenager, playing for silent films. It was right up his street, and would have been up mine too, had I been born a few decades earlier. He told me that he was once frantically playing away and the cinema manager called out, 'It's alright, sonny, you can stop now; they've all gone home!'

Our family attended the Methodist church, the spiritual influence of which passed me by as a child, certain other aspects making more of an impression. Mother was president of the Women's Meeting, and the mass gathering of her Tuesday afternoon flock produced such an aroma of lavender perfume, I can almost still smell it today. They seemed to have an abundance of what they called 'faith teas'. As a child I always thought this a rather odd phrase. It apparently meant that because you never knew what or how much people would bring, you would have to have faith that there would be enough to go round. This would have given the occasions a nice element of surprise, were it not for the fact that most people brought the same thing every time. I especially remember Dorothy's contribution of what she called her 'fish paste san-riches'.

As well as their faith teas, our church seemed to have an abundance of socials. These were jolly occasions, comprising of games, food and entertainment, and Dad, being chief organiser of the latter, often bribed me into playing.

When I was about nine, I was given a harmonica for Christmas. I endured a tantalising night, looking at it poking out of the top of my Christmas stocking on the end of my bed. When I could resist temptation no longer, and when I felt sure it must be morning, I pulled the harmonica out and started blowing. A voice came from across the landing: 'Put it back, it's only one o'clock!'

By Boxing Day I had devised a way of playing the piano and the harmonica at the same time. It involved wedging a stick under the piano lid with the harmonica attached to the end of it, thus freeing up both hands to play. Ingenious. Dad thought it might be a novel item for the church New Year's Eve social and I was duly put on the programme. I was to play a little tune I had made up. The audience buzzed in eager anticipation of 'young Susan's' innovative idea. I sat down at the piano and to my horror, the harmonica was poised six inches above my head. I'd not bargained for the church piano stool being lower than the one at home. In a flash, Mother appeared on the stage, armed with a pile of hymn books, on which she instructed me to sit, thus bringing my mouth in line with the harmonica. She beamed at the audience, thanked them for their forbearance and returned to her seat amid rapturous applause. Since she had now stolen the show, I saw little point in carrying on, but fought back the tears, played my tune and when I got home, chucked the whole jolly lot in the dustbin.

At the age of ten, I was the youngest child to be awarded a Hampshire County Music Exhibition – this achievement being entirely due, I might add, to the inspirational teaching of the wonderful Mary Brutnell. The award meant that, from then on, all my tuition fees were paid for. Two years later, all eight piano grades were done and dusted, so I didn't deplete the County's coffers for too long. Award-winners' concerts were held in Winchester and Mother and I always took a picnic lunch to eat in the park before the event. I looked forward to this more than the concert, the latter being a rather nerve-wracking ordeal. Dad always insisted that it was good to be nervous because it showed you cared. Really?!

My father was the church choirmaster and organist at Trinity Methodist Church, Basingstoke, for sixty years. His sensitive playing was much appreciated, as was his sense of humour. He was particularly adept at playing such tunes as 'Happy Birthday' or 'Anniversary Waltz' (and even Cliff Richard's 'Congratulations' when someone got engaged), disguising them in the style of Bach and managing to keep a straight face to boot.

Dad was also a local preacher, often taking services in the villages on a Sunday afternoon. From the age of eleven I used to go with him and play for the hymns – it got me out of the washing up. Sometimes there was a piano (usually a pretty awful one) and sometimes a harmonium, but I particularly remember going to Cliddesden church, where a little old lady pumped the organ with a great long lever in order to get the air into the pipes. If her energy levels were low after a big Sunday lunch, she used to say, 'Oh, the hymns is gonna dribble out today my duck!'

I used to go with Dad to Wootton St Lawrence Methodist Chapel, which rarely had a congregation of more than five, two of whom were sisters. The Wootton Sisters, as we called them, were well-bred ladies with blue-rinsed hair, who took their roles very seriously. One was in charge of welcoming people at the door (in the unlikely event of anyone entering it) and giving out the hymn books. The other read the lesson and took up the offering. It was all very cosy and rather lovely.

'You must teach! You must teach!'

On arriving at secondary school, it was a nasty shock to discover that the head of music was none other than my first piano teacher! Our frosty relationship resumed. She used to disappear into the cupboard on the pretext of looking for some music and we would see cigarette smoke curling underneath the door. She used to ask the class a question, ending with the words, 'And don't bother to put your hand up, Susan Fleming; I'm not asking you.' She seemed to resent my knowing the answers and turned my best subject into my least enjoyable. However, justice finally prevailed! On my last day at school, she sat at the piano to play the school hymn for the leavers' service and someone had put drawing pins on the hammers. Now, who would have done a thing like that?

Secondary school held no attraction for me whatsoever. I enjoyed sport, music, art and English, but, in my considered opinion, history was boring and geography only relevant if you wanted to be an air hostess. As for maths, that was something I just couldn't get my head round. It seemed to me that you either had the ability to understand it or you hadn't. I definitely hadn't, and as I saw little point in trying to force a talent for the subject, I often utilised the lesson time by practising the fingering of double-thirds scales on my desk. The teacher once spotted me and suggested that if I wished to practise the piano I should go to the music room and do it properly. His remark was intended as sarcasm but I didn't need a second invitation. I was off!

Being a pianist can be a pretty solitary affair. You miss out on the fun and the challenge of playing with others. There was a spare violin kicking around at home, so I decided to book myself in for lessons at school, thinking how wonderful it would be if they happened to clash with maths lessons on the timetable.

(They didn't.) We weren't taught individually, but five of us had to cram together in a tiny room where we could scarcely breathe, let alone play. Our teacher was a peripatetic (love that word) who shared our frustration at being put in what would more accurately be described as a cupboard.

It wasn't her fault. However, one day her frustration reached such a pitch that she lost her temper, flung her arms in the air and sent all our bows flying. Mine hit the ceiling, then ricocheted down into my eye, doing quite a lot of damage. Thus ended my days of being on the fiddle.

As a child, I had often sat and watched my father play the big old pipe organ at church, marvelling how he could manage to coordinate each hand on two different manuals and pedal with his feet (without looking) all at the same time. It seemed, to me, to present the same challenge as patting your head with one hand and rubbing your tummy with the other, which, as we all know, is jolly difficult. Then, of course, you had to control the swell pedal and pull stops out – either individually or by means of pistons that you operated with your feet. These shot out various combinations of stops automatically and I found them absolutely fascinating. When I became a teenager, with legs long enough to reach the pedals, I didn't want to watch Dad – I wanted to do it myself!

Being the organist's daughter, I was given permission to practise the organ any time I liked – and I liked nothing more. On Saturdays, when my friends were getting their buzz from tester pots on the make-up counter of Woolworths, I was getting mine from sitting at this great instrument and pulling out all the stops, revelling at the power I had at my fingertips to fill every corner of the building with such incredible sound.

I was self-taught and, as such, was probably doing a lot of things the wrong way. However, I was good enough to play for weddings and funerals – with the added incentive of getting paid.

The organ was high up and had a 'rear view mirror' positioned over it so you could see what was happening down below. There was an elderly spinster at church, called Susie Clark, who made it her business to be at weddings to ensure everything went smoothly. When I was much younger I had visited her house and seen piles of dentures on the table. I couldn't think why she could possibly need so many teeth when she only had one mouth, but Mother said not to be worried: she made dentures for a living. I thought that very strange.

As it turned out, several years later the false teeth lady and I were often at the church together for weddings. The deal was that when the bride was ready to come down the aisle, Susie Clark would wave her handkerchief as a signal to me to begin the wedding march. On one occasion I was playing merrily away, when I spotted the hanky-waving routine in the mirror. Goodness, the bride was ten minutes early! I launched into the 'Wedding March', looked in the mirror and could see no bride. What I did see, however, was the false teeth lady frantically waving her hands for me to stop. She had a cold and had pulled a handkerchief out of her pocket to blow her nose.

Then there was the Christmas wedding: seeing the handkerchief in the mirror, I started up 'Here comes the bride'. But come she did not. I played it again. Still no sign of her. I then decided to improvise around the theme. (This is something organists do when they want to look a bit clever and by this time I was looking a bit stupid.) It wasn't my fault but I was feeling rather exposed. I was just considering the possibility that I might be going to witness a bridegroom jilted at the altar, when the bride emerged down the aisle in fits of giggles. Apparently, her veil had become caught in a holly decoration at the church door and, in their desperation to set her free, the bridesmaids had made the situation worse and got her well and truly tangled up.

Isn't it interesting how emotional it's possible to get at weddings, even when one doesn't know the couple from Adam?

I always had a lump in my throat. Funerals were even worse, and quite an ordeal to play for as a teenager, but I needed the money. I shall never forget the funeral where the vicar opened with the words: 'We are gathered here today to witness the marriage . . .' I doubt that he will ever forget it either.

In my teenage years I spent a good deal of time at Basingstoke's Haymarket Theatre, playing for artists who needed a pianist. One such celebrity was a person called Cyril Fletcher, who came to do a one-man show. I had never heard of him. (If you have, best keep quiet and not show your age.) We rehearsed in the afternoon and he informed me that I was to play his signature tune as he came onto the stage. He positioned himself in the wings and called, 'Ok? Let's roll.' I froze. He called again, 'Ok?' Well, no, clearly not. I was only sixteen, no one had provided me with any music and I sat at the piano, terrified. He stormed onto the stage and yelled, 'Don't tell me I've been given a pianist who doesn't even know my signature tune!'

To my great surprise I heard myself say, 'You hum it and I'll play it.' He gave a withering look, and hummed it. I gave a smile of relief and played it. That seemed to reassure him that I could be trusted and from then on we got on just fine.

Outside school I was doing classical concerts, playing jazz in restaurants, writing concert reviews for the local newspaper and enjoying being in a grown-up world. Back in the classroom, I felt I didn't fit, and couldn't wait to get out. There was no way I was going to hang around to do A levels, but what was I to do instead? My sister Maggie had trained as a nursery nurse and it seemed a sensible qualification to have under one's belt. Yes, I would do that. When I conveyed my intentions to the headmistress she practically exploded.

'That is not a career! Do you want to be playing nursery rhymes all day? You must use your music, young lady. You must teach! You must teach!' No, my mind was made up. I left her office with her final words on the subject ringing in my ear: 'Susan Fleming, I wash my hands of you!'

I was interviewed by Mrs Jordan, the principal of a nursery training college near Reading. She was an incredibly small, mouse-like lady, with a very tiny voice to match. I felt a bit like a giant by comparison, which gave me a kind of confidence. It was eleven years since my sister had been at the college, but Mrs Jordan remembered her. Indeed, despite her diminutive appearance, it struck me that Mrs Jordan probably didn't miss a trick. Maggie had been Student of the Year and as I left, the Principal's little bird-like eyes twinkled and her tiny voice squeaked, 'Miss Fleming, your reputation goes before you.'

I used to walk from my home to the station, take the seven a.m. train from Basingstoke to Reading, then a bus to college one week and to a nursery on alternate weeks. The course itself wasn't academically difficult – in fact, most of it was just common sense – but nursery weeks especially were jolly hard work and very tiring. I, too, won the Student of the Year award, and have always wondered whether they were being kind or whether it was genuinely merited.

So here I was, aged eighteen, a qualified nursery nurse and, apart from playing nursery rhymes, I wasn't using my music. What should I do now? My sister had gone on to work on Cunard liners but that didn't appeal to me. I must teach. I must teach! I realised that I must also eat humble pie, and wrote to my old headmistress with the news that I had been offered a place at teacher training college. Her reply was kind and encouraging. She didn't say, 'I told you so', but I'm pretty sure she was thinking it.

College by the sea

Weymouth Teacher Training College, affiliated to Southampton University, was by no means at the top of the league but it was by the sea, which, as far as I was concerned, was much more important. The swimming, the sailing, the sunbathing were wonderful distractions from one's studies. The lure of the beach was difficult to resist; even more so was the lure of the sailors at Portland, as many students discovered. I wasn't one of them. No, honestly.

At last I was doing what came naturally: using my music. Of the ten people in my year doing the music course, I was the only one majoring in composition. This meant I was often sent off to schools to try out things I had written for children. On one occasion I was accosted by a little girl who queried that I was a composer, because she didn't think I looked like one. When I asked her what a composer did look like, she chirruped, 'Dead', and skipped off. Fair point.

I was very fortunate to have been given a car by my parents in my second year. They were keen that I should be independent and not be at the mercy of other people's dubious driving skills. Unlike students of today, very few had their own transport, and those of us who did suddenly found ourselves rather popular.

Having wheels meant that I was able to take myself off and sit with my manuscript book in the beautiful Dorset countryside, scribbling away as inspiration flowed and tunes filled my head. I loved to spend whole days just revelling in being alone, being creative. When it came to writing lyrics, I was grateful for having inherited my father's passion for words. What I didn't know then was that I would one day be given a gift of words from my heavenly father, to use for his glory.

I started college with every intention of going to church, but after a few months of creeping out of the hostel on a Sunday morning, trying not to wake those who were sleeping off their Saturday night, I succumbed. I wanted to be in with the crowd, and the crowd was heading for the pub, not the church. I didn't want to be different. I drank beer (or scrumpy, even worse), started smoking (shocking) and thus embarked on what I thought of as 'a holiday from Jesus', having convinced myself that he wouldn't mind.

No one at home was aware of the cigarettes – or so I thought. I used to work in my bedroom and puff away with the window wide open. One day Mother came up to my room for something and as she left she said, 'By the way, it does make the whole house draughty when you blow your smoke out of the window.' Heavens! She knew! Her words hit me with far more impact than any amount of lecturing would have done. She was one wise woman. Sadly, I was not; I continued the ghastly habit until I became a Christian. It then dawned on me that I was guilty of the equivalent of lighting a bonfire in church because my body was the temple of the Holy Spirit. I gave it up.

When I was a student, I spent Sunday evenings playing keyboard with a trad jazz group called The Wey Valley Stompers. This gave me a chance to vent the jazz bent I had to suppress during the week's classical training. We played in a hotel on the seafront called The Victoria, known locally as The Vic. There were six in the band; I was the only female and was teased mercilessly.

For my finals I had to write a string quartet. It had four movements and was a very time-consuming task. These days I use a computer programme for composing; in those days it all had to be written by hand – and be legible. I was fortunate in having a very understanding room-mate who didn't mind me having the light on until two in the morning. My tutor found four willing string players who were a great encouragement and they came and played the piece to my examiner. They subsequently performed the quartet at a concert in aid of Salisbury Cathedral, where it was recorded, together with someone's persistent cough.

Shortly before my finals, my tutor reminded me that the exam would include a performance on my second instrument. This was a slight problem as I wasn't aware I had to have one. What I did have, however, was a good friend, Mike, who was a classical guitarist. For this purpose, he had very short nails on his left hand and very long ones on his right; his playing was brilliant and seemingly effortless and I could sit and listen to him for hours. In two months he somehow helped me progress from strumming four chords to playing a Bach fugue. There was a tricky little bit where I should have played an E but just couldn't reach it. Mike said that since it wasn't a well-known piece I would probably get away with substituting a C. I had no option but to risk it.

'Lovely, thank you,' said the examiner. 'It's not a very well-known fugue but it's one of my favourites.' That was it. I was done for. He continued, ' And what a good idea to substitute a C in that tricky little bit.'

I left college with a merit Diploma in Education. It was something I never thought I would achieve but, thankfully, my headmistress had thought otherwise. When I set about looking for a job, despite my plans to be independent, for some reason I ended up living back at home and teaching in Basingstoke. I didn't appreciate it then, but I now realise that this was the first indication of God knowing best, for only he knew what was in store for our family.

New big-innings
(marrying the cricketer)

My job as an infant teacher required me to teach all subjects in the morning and take class music lessons in my school and the junior school next door in the afternoon. It goes without saying that since mornings involved me feigning a knowledge of maths (I do wonder how I got away with it), I much preferred afternoons. I certainly wouldn't get away with anything these days, such are the rules and regulations of the teaching profession.

In those days teachers were allowed to use more of their own initiative and less of the government's. There were many more 'born teachers' and they got results by inspiring children rather than impressing Ofsted. The only officialdom I can remember was the occasional visit of an H.M.I. (Her Majesty's Inspector), and they were usually nothing to be frightened of. Once I had been doing some tie-dying with my class and had strung a length of string across the classroom and pegged all the pieces of material up to dry. The H.M.I. walked in, unannounced, and exclaimed, 'I seem to have arrived on washing day. How splendid!' These days one would probably be accused of breaking health and safety rules.

Coming back to my home town meant that I was able to quickly slot back into the old musical scene, whilst getting involved in some new ones. I was introduced to a young man called George, who conducted the local male voice choir. Both of us being pianists, we did the obvious thing and went out and bought some piano duets. We discovered that we 'clicked', totally, and there followed an amazing two years of concerts together. People were saying we were meant for each other, and indeed we were, musically. One evening, after a particularly well-received concert at Reading, and in a moment of euphoric madness, George proposed and I accepted. The local paper got wind of the news and ran a full-page article on what they called 'The Musical Duo Of The Year'. People we didn't even know sent us engagement presents and we were swept along in a great wave of excitement.

Only a few weeks into our engagement I realised that the excitement was in our well-wishers, but not in us. At the piano we could have set the world alight, but away from it there was no spark in the romantic sense. Looking back, I don't know why we ever thought it would work; it would probably have been a disaster. We would have played the piano all day and never done any housework! He was loathe to accept it, but I gave George his ring back. There was also the small matter of returning people's gifts, which was embarrassingly difficult. My parents were hugely relieved; they could see it wasn't right. When I asked why she hadn't said something, Mother just looked heavenward and simply said, 'I did.'

George and I remained friends. We still had several concert engagements to fulfil so we couldn't afford to fall out. After one concert, we decided to go on to a party that was being given by a friend. We arrived about eleven o' clock, and George being in tails and I in a long black dress, we were conspicuous to say the least. One audacious young man named Rob spotted me across the room and said to himself: 'That's the girl I'm going to marry!' He somehow found out my telephone number, rang it and persuaded me to meet him. He was different from any of my previous boyfriends – refreshingly so. He was very tall and skinny, well mannered, educated, not bad looking and had the added attraction of a sports car.

Marriage was the last thing on my agenda; however, I soon found myself more sure of this man than I had ever been of anything or anyone, and my agenda went swiftly out of the window. The vital 'spark' was evident to all, and, besides, Mother had also fallen for him, so that was that. We were engaged after two months, married four months later, and this time Mother's eyes were lifted heavenward in thankfulness.

A month before our wedding, I dragged Rob to the shops to buy some wedding shoes. When the assistant asked what size he was Rob looked rather blank, then muttered, 'um, eight? nine? nine and a half? I don't really know.' That much was pretty obvious.

Recognising the need for some female logic in the situation, I pitched in. 'Well, what size are the ones you have on?'

Rob whispered in my ear, 'Don't know, they're my Dad's.' I thought: this man sure does need a wife.

Rob has always had a great passion for cricket. Our wedding date, therefore, had to be fitted in around his match fixtures. The only available day, 26 August 1972, was a typical British summer one – chilly, overcast and very windy. Rob had come to the church in our best man's open-top sports car, and his godmother had greeted him with a kiss on his arrival. As I walked down the aisle he turned and smiled at me, his windswept hair sticking up all over the place and his left cheek embossed with bright red lipstick. I thought: well, at least he's in his own shoes.

He loved me more than cricket

He knelt on bended knee and said,
'Please will you marry me, Susie?'
I'd been proposed to twice before,
and I was rather choosy;
but this time I was certain
that I'd found my mate for life,
and six months after meeting,
we two were man and wife.

The book was signed, the deed was done
and Rob had won his bride.
For better or for worse? Who knew?
Who cared? He beamed with pride.

He'd won his maiden over,
there would be no sticky wicket,
because he knew – yes, it was true –
he loved me more than cricket!

Mother

We began married life in a beautiful cottage at Lindford. near Farnham. It belonged to some friends who had gone to Ghana for a year and we looked after it, plus two donkeys, rent-free. It was quite a way to travel to our teaching jobs in Basingstoke but it was all very idyllic and we felt very fortunate.

Since we were both travelling to work in the same direction we obviously didn't need two cars. We decided to keep my beloved Morris 1000 convertible and sell Rob's Triumph Spitfire, knowing we would get a better price for his. We put an advertisement in the local newspaper, with my mother's telephone as a contact number. When we asked if there had been any enquiries Mum said, 'Only someone wanting an aeroplane. I told him he must have the wrong number.'

My mother and I were very close; I adored her. A gracious lady with twinkling blue eyes and the loveliest smile, she had a warmth that touched people's hearts the minute they met her. She was no academic but she had incredible wisdom, on the subject of which she once famously said, 'You don't need a PhD to be wise; you just need to know the Lord.' My father commented, 'Do you know what a PhD is, dear?' to which she replied, 'Haven't got a clue.' (But, as you now know, she was pretty clued up about aeroplanes.)

Mother was an amazing Christian and was, as far as I was concerned, the only example I needed to follow in life. I saw no need to put my faith in a remote, invisible God, and chose to ignore Mum's comment that she wouldn't be with me for ever, that there was only one person who would be. I would cross that unthinkable bridge when I came to it.

In February 1973, Mother was admitted to hospital for tests after experiencing stomach pains. A few days later, the school secretary came into my classroom and said my father had just phoned. She didn't explain why, but just said she would take over the class and I must go to my parents' house. When I arrived, Rob was there. He had also been summoned. To my surprise, Mum was there too; she had been discharged, and I took that to be a good sign. It didn't for one minute occur to me that it could be a bad one. But it was. Mother had been sent home from hospital because there was nothing they could do for her. She sat us down and calmly said, 'It's cancer, my darlings, apparently. I have three weeks to live.' I froze, and she continued, 'Don't worry, I said to the doctor, I shall need much longer than that: my husband can't even boil an egg!'

Nothing, but nothing could have prepared me for this moment. That unthinkable bridge had come, and somehow it would have to be crossed. I looked at my father, strong and protective, standing beside her. I looked at my mother and she was smiling. Smiling! How could they be like that? How could they be so accepting? I didn't understand any of it. I had always assumed that Mum would be there to see my children born, to be a part of their lives; indeed, it occurred to me that I had made an awful lot of assumptions, which God had now cruelly shattered.

Later that evening, Mother suggested we all played Scrabble. She said it would help take our minds off 'it'. I doubted that anything could possibly distract my mind from such devastating news.' Now', she announced, 'I don't want you to make allowances for me just because I'm ill.' Guess who won?

Mother belonged to a prayer group, which rejoiced in the splendid name of The Holy Hens, and there wasn't a day when one of them didn't come clucking to our house, bringing food, fellowship and flowers – the latter in such abundance, we could easily have been mistaken for a florist's. Barney Coombes, pastor of the local Baptist Church, loved coming to visit. He said to me one day, 'It always happens. I come to minister to her and it's she who ministers to me!'

The stream of visitors was endless and Rob and I had never seen such generosity and caring before. These Christians had certainly got something. However, grateful as I was for their love and encouragement, I was also troubled by it because I didn't want them giving Mum false hopes. It was all very confusing. According to initial estimates, she had only a few days to live, yet here she was looking radiant. Even her doctor was bewildered. Not known for his tactful bedside manner, he exclaimed, 'Well, Mrs Fleming, you're determined not to perish, aren't you.'

Her blue eyes twinkling at the very thought, she replied, 'Oh, I shan't be doing that anyway, doctor!'

In her diary on 7 March Mum had written, 'Doctor not very hopeful but God is in control.' On 4 May her entry read, 'My specialist is mystified. I should be getting worse and I'm getting better! To God be the glory!' Convinced by her buoyant condition that there may be a point in operating after all, her specialist took her back into hospital, but his investigations revealed that the cancer, far from abating, had in fact spread. Her fame had also spread and the nurses would bring young cancer patients, who weren't coping very well, to chat with her. I thought this was a bit much but she, of course, counted it a privilege.

A great many people, all over the world, were praying for Mother to be healed and I felt guilty that I was sceptical. She sensed this and said she would definitely be healed; it just may not be for our eyes to see. Mother adored Rob's voice and often asked him to sit beside her bed and read the Bible to her - a bit of a crafty move on her part, but she was never one to miss an opportunity.

Her favourite Bible verse was Romans 8, verse 28: 'We know that all things work together for good for those who love God, who are called according to his purpose'. What is more, she held to that belief right to the end. From where I was standing, she would have been justified in doubting it. I certainly did. I still couldn't understand how she could be so peaceful. She used to say, 'The peace of God that passes all understanding: I now know what that means because I have it.'

It wasn't three weeks; it was three months. They were a steep learning curve for Dad in the kitchen, and his culinary skills improved far beyond egg-boiling. More importantly, those final weeks were the most significant of any that had gone before, not only in Mum's life but in our lives as well. For what we saw in her was the grace of God at work, and working so powerfully that we could neither deny nor ignore it. Her inner peace, her radiance, amazed everyone, and her trust in God remained unshaken to the end.

On 31 May 1973, aged sixty-two, Laura Fleming was promoted to glory; a glory so richly deserved. She had shown us how to live, then she had shown us how to die. God had done wonderful things in her life and then he did an even more wonderful thing by staying the hand of suffering and taking her home to be with him. It wasn't for our eyes to see, but he healed her, completely. I can say that now because I believe it. I couldn't have said it at the time, however, because I was cross. I was cross with the doctor for wasting time with his initial misdiagnosis of indigestion, I was cross with God for taking her too soon, I was cross that she would never know my children, I was just cross all round.

The last thing Mother said to Rob and me was, 'If I have to die for you two to become Christians, then I'm on my way!' But I didn't want to know, thank you very much. I had big questions, and the biggest was this: you can dispose of a body, but where do you put the soul? All that loveliness, all that compassion, all the qualities that God had planted and nurtured in Mother over the years — where were they going to go? Her spirit, the very essence of who she was and what God had made her, surely that couldn't be just snuffed out? It seemed to me that heaven was the most logical resting place for such things, but I still had to deal with my crossness.

I went back to school two weeks after Mum died and, with hindsight, that was too soon. I wasn't coping very well. One of my fellow teachers, Doreen Gray, was a lovely Christian, and she told me it was okay to be cross. Then she said that, in her experience, God doesn't always stop things, but he always uses them. I have never forgotten her words, and many times since then, have had cause to realise the truth of them. Mum's last words rang in my ears. She had been right, again (even without a PhD). She was willing for God to use her because she knew that greater are the plans of him who sees it all . . .

Death

Death: it is the only thing of which we can be sure.
There will be no escaping it, we shall be here no more.
It's really quite bizarre to think one day our heart will stop,
and we'll be put into a box with flowers on the top.
And people at our funeral will give tributes with such grace
and say nice things. (How sad they'd never said them to our face.)

Our body will be buried in some gloomy graveyard plot
or cremated in a furnace. Done and dusted. That's your lot.
Yes, death's the only thing in life of which we can be certain.
We'll shuffle off this mortal coil and go beyond that curtain.
And here we have a problem: just when will our end come?
We hope it will be later but it's all too soon for some.

Death's a subject we avoid discussing as a rule.
All that hell fire and damnation stuff just sounds a trifle cruel.
But what exactly happens to we humans when we die?
Do we all grow wings and float around like angels in the sky?
Do we pop our clogs and plunge into eternity's black hole?
You can get rid of a body, but where do you put the soul?

Some people turn their back on God and tell him to get lost.
They'll think about him later, that won't matter (fingers crossed).
They've pleased themselves and lived a life
where Jesus hasn't reigned
and think of heaven as a place where entry can be gained.
They reckon they have done enough good deeds to get them in
and God will really be impressed and overlook their sin.

If you knew you'd die tomorrow, how would the prospect feel?
Do you think you'd go to heaven or to hell? 'Cos both are real.
Death will come to all of us, of that we can be sure.
Why risk hell when there's a heaven
where there's life for evermore?!

Oh, heaven is a party but it's not a free-for-all,
It's especially for people who've responded to God's call.
Repentance is the password that will get us through the gate.
We must deal with it today – tomorrow might just be too late.

Rob didn't come from a church-going family but he had been confirmed as a teenager, and imagined that was all you had to do to qualify as a Christian. Having been brought up in a family where church played such a central part, I was equally guilty of assuming that was all that was necessary. But we both discovered that it's rather like thinking you are in love (which I did, plenty of times). When you do eventually meet the right person and are faced with the real thing, you realise that what you previously thought was love, actually wasn't.

We were beginning to realise that Mother was right when she had said she wouldn't be around for ever; there was only one person who would be. Putting our faith in a Christlike human being was not how it worked; trying to be like them was not how it happened; getting into heaven on their ticket was not an option. We realised what we had previously thought was faith, was not, because now we were faced with the real thing.

One Sunday morning, a few weeks after Mother died, I woke up with a strong conviction that we should go to church. I prodded my snoring husband and said, 'Let's go to South Warnborough Church today.'

He wasn't too thrilled at such a rude awakening, pointing out that it was some miles away (we now lived in West Liss), we didn't know what time the service was and, actually, he wasn't really awake yet. 'Why South Warnborough?' he mumbled. It was where a few of Mother's Holy Hens went and that seemed a good enough reason to me. We went. Having been brought up in the Methodist church where services started at eleven o clock, I naively assumed that to be the norm and we turned up at five minutes to, half an hour late.

The heavy oak door gave a hideous creak as we pushed it open and we were on the point of running off in embarrassment, when the vicar's wife swiftly left her pew and came and gave us such a welcome embrace that an escape was now simply out of the question. After the service we were taken to the vicarage and weren't allowed to go home until midnight, by which time we realised that we had just spent the day with two of the most amazing people we had ever come across. Gray and Judy Sutherland were to become very precious friends.

It is very special when both people in a marriage come to faith at the same time, and Rob and I were now on the road together. It was a relief to discover that Christians (contrary to my father-in-law's opinion) are quite normal people. They don't have to stop having fun, they don't have to wear frumpy clothes, they don't have to be teetotal, they don't even have to go to church every single Sunday if they don't want to (but now we did want to). It was to my great shame and sadness that I hadn't taken Jesus seriously earlier in my life. Mother and I could have shared even more.

Babies, blessings
and the booze ban

When Mother was ill, the headmistress at the school where I taught kindly allowed me to work just in the mornings so that I could look after Mum in the afternoons. Dad was with Mum in the mornings and worked just in the afternoons. It was a good system. By the time Mother died I had begun to rather enjoy teaching part-time and (choosing my moment carefully) I asked Rob if I could carry on doing so. To my surprise, he suggested I gave up work altogether! Mindful of how understanding and generous my headmistress had been, I felt slightly bad at telling her of my intention. She asked why I was leaving. 'Because Rob says I can,' was clearly not an acceptable reason. She said she didn't want to lose me and I would have to come up with a better excuse than that. Four months later, I returned to her office, patted my pregnant tummy and she had to agree that, as excuses go, I now had a pretty good one.

Our first baby was due a year to the very day after Mum died. Thankfully, it was eleven days late – I think I would have found the anniversaries hard to cope with. I was absolutely certain it would be a girl and we would call her Laura. It was, and we did. She brought us great joy, and continues to do so.

Soon after Laura was born we were on the move again, this time to a large former rectory at Winchfield in Hampshire. The Church Commission needed someone to look after it until it was sold off, and a friend had suggested us. It was rent-free and we couldn't believe how lucky we were.

The Not-so-reverend Hare

We once lived in a house
that was a former Rectory.
The Church Commission asked us
to look after it, rent–free.

We rattled round its fourteen rooms
and Rob liked to pretend
that he was the incumbent
(naughty man) and one weekend
a couple asked the 'Reverend Hare'
to baptise their new son.
Did this vicar tell them
he was not a proper one?

He did not. I heard him say
'I'd be delighted, come inside.'
This unsuspecting pair
were being taken for a ride!
Eventually he did come clean;
they may have thought him odd,
instead of which they saw
the funny side of it,
thank God.

The day we moved into the Rectory, we found we needed a screwdriver. (We had our own in a box but couldn't remember which one. After six house moves we are now experts and have learnt the wisdom of sticky labels.) We popped over the road and knocked on the door of our new neighbours, Lynne and John Blay. Within minutes we just knew that we were going to get on famously, and after forty years they are still two of our greatest friends.

When Lynne gave her life to Jesus she announced that she knew what she would have to go out and buy. I was expecting her to say a Bible but she came out with, 'A diary; you Christians are so busy!' I bought the Bible; she bought the diary – the Christian's second essential book.

After eighteen months we moved to a small bungalow in South Warnborough. It was owned by a dear old lady, known to everyone as Granny Mabel, who was the widow of a Canon. Judy had told us about it and we made an appointment to go and see it. We had barely set foot in the place when Granny Mabel asked if we wanted it. We said it might be nice to look round it first. 'Very well,' she said. 'You look round, I'll get you a sherry and then we can decide.' Rob has an eye for spotting potential and on this occasion had to spot it jolly quickly. When Granny Mabel returned to the room, we told her we should like to buy the bungalow. She had previously only lived in church accommodation, the bungalow was the only home she had owned and she had got it into her head that a sale was somehow not quite legal unless you went to an estate agent. We assured her it wasn't necessary; we would buy it privately and save her the agent's fees. However, she was adamant and the next day a For Sale board went up. Bless her.

Shortly after the move our second daughter, Charlotte, was born. We were thrilled to have another girl, although Laura's hopes of having a brother were dashed. Thankfully, her disappointment was short-lived; she decided sisters were okay and the two of them have been great friends ever since.

Our move to the village coincided with an influx of Christians from London. They had all been on their spiritual journey rather longer than us, we learnt a lot from them and they soon became very special friends. One couple, Gordon and Sally Scutt, held fortnightly meetings in their converted granary. I played the piano for these and they were wonderful times of fellowship, attracting many Christians from the surrounding villages. On one occasion there were more than a hundred people and, since the granary was perched on staddle stones, we rather feared we might all disappear through the floor.

On one Granary Evening, the last song was 'What a friend we have in Jesus'. I played it 'straight' for the first verse, found that a trifle boring, so jazzed up the remainder. When the meeting was over, Gordon came up to me and gently said, 'I could tell that you were enjoying that, but remember we are here to see Jesus, not Susie Hare.' I obviously wasn't meaning to draw attention to myself, but conceded that it may have looked like it. I took his words on board.

That evening at the granary was a real turning point for me, a moment when I realised that what I had thought of as my talent was actually God's gift. It suddenly hit me that my whole attitude was going to have to change. After years of taking the credit, hearing the applause, feeling the pride, I knew that from now on the glory must go to him.

When I got home that evening, I decided I wanted to write my first song for the Lord. Not being quite sure how to go about it, I just opened the Bible and hoped for the best. It opened at Numbers 6, verses 24 to 26: 'The Lord bless you and keep you; the Lord make his face to shine upon you, and be gracious to you; the Lord lift up his countenance upon you, and give you peace.' Those words seemed to be as good as any, so I quickly wrote a tune to go with them and went to bed. That very simple song, which was subsequently published in *Songs of Fellowship*, sold more than any I have ever written, is still selling and is apparently very popular in Australia. Eight more songs found their way into *Songs of Fellowship,* and I made the amazing discovery that when God inspired me to write, I didn't have to strive; all I had to do was wait on him and make sure I always had manuscript paper in my pocket.

Armed with this assurance of divine assistance, I decided to embark on a musical based on the prodigal son. The cast comprised seventy young people and a few adults from local churches and we had tremendous fun. We put on two performances in the village hall and another at Basingstoke Methodist Church. The production included a boozy party scene, into which our young people threw themselves with great enthusiasm and quite a few bottles. However, the Methodists, being Methodists, had requested that the scene be toned down and no bottles be evident. There were a few tantrums in the troupe but we agreed to comply. Imagine my horror, therefore, when the curtain went up on scene three, and the partygoers came staggering onto the stage brandishing bottles and hiccupping wildly. It has to be said, it was a pretty good interpretation of what the Bible calls 'riotous living'. We later discovered that an amateur dramatic society had put on a show at the hall on the previous evening and had left some props in the wings. The props in question just happened to be beer bottles and our lot gleefully assumed the booze ban had been lifted. Oops.

A few years down the line, when I began to have my musicals published, I was sometimes asked to attend performances up and down the country (the furthest up was Scotland but I didn't go). A church in Stroud put on my Easter musical, a very ambitious, two-and-a-half hour undertaking for a small church, with lots of 'doubling-up' of parts.

A lady bustled to the front before curtain up and, in a rich Gloucestershire accent, announced that the composer was in the audience and she hoped I would be pleased with their effort. She continued, 'Now, Mrs 'are, unfortunately Terry was tooken ill with stomach pains on Thursday and he's in 'ospital now, so Joseph of Arimathea will 'ave to be a woman. We 'ope you don't mind.' Of course I didn't mind (any more than I minded the centurion also being the wrong gender); I just felt sorry for poor old Terry having to miss out after months of rehearsal.

With mother on my 21st birthday

Wedding day

Mark, Naomi, Jacob and Laura

Mark, Rhys, Jed, Owen and Charlie

On holiday with Gray and Judy

With my prayer group friends

Laura and Charlie

Rob and me – Ruby Wedding Day

At the piano

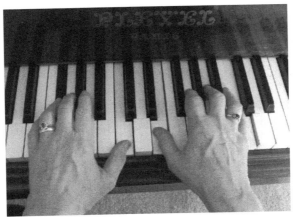

Hands on

One Sunday I sat down to play

One Sunday I sat down to play
my piano, and I found
that when I touched a certain note
there was a clonking sound.

The clonk was really pretty bad
and I was at a loss
to know what might be causing it.
It made me rather cross.

The piano tuner came and said,
'This piano's old; ideally
it should be reconditioned,
which will cost a bomb, but really,

if you've got five thousand pounds to spare,
it would be worth your while.'
Five thousand pounds? I was aghast,
and then I saw him smile.

'But there is an alternative
which won't cost you a thing:
inside there's a harmonica
that's bouncing on the string.

To save yourself the money
I should take that out instead.'
We're pretty sure who put it there:
that rascal grandson, Jed.

Busy, busy, busy

By now we were very involved in the Christian scene and life was incredibly busy. Lynne was right about the diary.

The organist at South Warnborough was an elderly lady who had been stalwart for many years. If we are being honest, her attribute of faithfulness rather outshone her talent for playing, but the village couldn't have done without her. One day she announced that she would like to be released from playing for family services. These services were apparently becoming a little more than she could cope with. Added to which, Gray's penchant for doing things differently and spontaneously, whilst the rest of us loved it, threw her slightly off course.

So I was invited to take over the organ stool once a month, thus increasing the likelihood of even more spontaneity. Family services became popular, except in the opinion of a brigadier, who wrote a lengthy letter of complaint to Gray, stating that 'Last Sunday's service was an absolute pantomime.' He concluded his correspondence with the words, 'What is more, you forgot to pray for the Queen.' Shame on us.

An exposure to loud noises (could have been air rifles or the kids shouting, or even family services, I guess) resulted in Rob's hearing becoming quite a problem and he was finding teaching increasingly difficult. A friend of ours who owned a tennis court company offered Rob a job, and to my surprise he took it.

His knowledge of tennis was scant to say the least (he didn't even own a racket), but apparently that wouldn't be an issue. Family life was suddenly rather different. The children were usually in bed before Rob was home, there were no long school holidays – we all had to adjust. On the plus side, we did have a company car and Rob, in a rash moment, bought a second pair of shoes, the right size and all his own.

After five years, we had completed our plans for the bungalow and increased its market value. We had no great urgency to move but decided to put it up for sale and just see what happened. It sold within a week. We put in an offer on a cottage in Upton Grey, a couple of miles away. It meant more DIY but we were becoming pretty proficient now and couldn't wait to get cracking. To our dismay, we were gazzumped (by John Profumo, no less) and rendered homeless. However, Sally and Gordon just happened to have an empty cottage on their land and offered it to us for as long as it took to find another place. I must confess, we loved it there so much we didn't exactly hurry to find somewhere else. It was two years before we eventually moved a couple of miles up the road to the house where we still live.

Not a day goes by when we don't thank God for blessing us with a lovely house and beautiful garden which we love to share with our many friends.

Quite soon after we moved in, I started to get chest pains and was diagnosed with myocarditis – a disease which attacks the lining of the heart. The infection had also spread to the lining of my lungs and it was agony. I was in bed for a month, out of bed but very weak for the second month and not allowed to drive until after the third month. Altogether rather inconvenient of me, when there was so much to do. But the Christian network swung into action and all bases were miraculously covered, all school runs undertaken, all meals provided, and all washing, ironing and cleaning done. The house had never been so immaculate. I used to lie in bed and hear people let themselves in, do the hoovering, then leave. Half the time I didn't know who was doing what, but I was so grateful for all the love and practical help.

When I began to feel stronger, Rob and I felt it was decision time. We had been very busy 'giving out' and thought we should now 'receive'. We also felt that our daughters had outgrown the village Sunday school (lovely as it was) and we should be looking for a church where they could grow and mature in their faith. We found the very thing – St Mary's in Basingstoke. It was lively, the people were friendly, their children's work was good, and as we opened the leaflet we were given on arrival, we read that they were looking for an organist. Alex Ross, the vicar, fully appreciated that I needed to rest and didn't want to commit to anything too soon. He promised to not mention the word organist for six months. Alex was famous for having the kind of grin that made it impossible to refuse him anything, and six months later, to the very day, he grinned at me . . .

The organ at St Mary's was a lovely one and I enjoyed playing it. The children were receiving good teaching and Rob occasionally did the children's talk or read the lesson. We all felt at home and Laura once remarked, 'It feels very warm in our church, Mummy, and I don't think it's the radiators.'

The warmth of fellowship at St Mary's meant a lot to us. How good it is to recognise one's brothers and sisters by the spiritual genes we share from the same Father. The Christian family is an extensive one and we have lots more relations to meet yet! Friends have always been very important and special to us and we have a great many of them. My parents-in-law were always amazed by the vast number, their circle of friends being very small by comparison. I think it would be true to say that God has graciously bestowed on us the gift of hospitality. This demonstrates his sense of humour, since he knows full well how much I hate cooking! Rob's parents could never quite get their heads around the fact that we entertain a lot. We once ran an eight-week church Marriage Course, which involved having couples to our home (some of whom we'd not even met), giving them supper, watching a video and answering any questions they might have.

My mother-in-law and I had a conversation that went something like this:

'So let me get this right: you have people in your house whom you don't know from Adam?

'Yes.'

'Then you feed them?'

'We do.'

'Then they watch your television?'

'That's right.'

'Do they pay you, dear?'

'No.'

'Well, how extraordinary.'

To us, it was completely natural. To my in-laws it was completely nuts. I sometimes felt they viewed us with a degree of pity, convinced that we had been brainwashed by the God Squad.

Rob's mother was a very dear lady, whom we all adored. Very sadly, she had been a paraplegic since she was in her thirties, but she rarely complained and Rob's father – despite his atheism – was actually a bit of a saint. Although it is not how we viewed it, Ma saw her condition as being some kind of divine punishment (for what, we never established) and kept on the right side of the Almighty by having Communion once a month, brought to her by the local vicar. It was tempting (but unfair) to dismiss his visits as just a ritual. They were quite possibly significant for her but they were never commented on. Just before her eightieth birthday she announced that if anyone wanted to know what to give her, she would like a Bible. Once we had got over the shock of her request, we went out and bought her a splendid one, and threw in some daily Bible notes whilst we were at it. How sad that it's so much easier to share one's faith with complete strangers than with those in one's own family. We regret our reticence.

Life continued to be full, and my memories of the next few years seem to have been submerged under the heading of 'teenage taxi service'. Living in the sticks, we didn't have the luxury of public transport, apart from one bus to Basingstoke on a Tuesday (and presumably back again), and spent much of our time ferrying our daughters to their various activities. However, there was an advantage to this: we knew exactly where they were going, because we took them there, and we knew exactly what time they were coming back because we fetched them. In short, we knew exactly what they were up to. They didn't much like it, of course, but now they have children of their own, I notice they are saying precisely the same thing.

More time

You want to spend more time with him
but somehow in your day,
all the things you're busy with keep getting in the way.
You really want to listen but there's so much in your week,
often, when you're rushing round, it's hard to hear him speak.
You want to find a moment to be quiet with your Lord
but, somehow, things like sitting down keep going by the board.

Your resolution each New Year is always to do less;
but then, in next to no time, your diary's in a mess,
and life goes madly hurtling on, at much too fast a pace:
there's never any let-up and there's never any space.
The list of things to do, it seems, is one that has no end;
you're shopping and you're cooking, entertaining each weekend,
and then you have to iron his shirts and scrub the jolly floor;
you're being 'just a housewife' but you wish you could be more.

And all the while you fix a smile around the kitchen sink,
you wish you had a moment to fix yourself a drink …
You ought to read the Bible, but you know the kind of thing –
you've just found Zephaniah and the telephone will ring;
you're hearing people's problems as they sob them
down the phone
and wish you could admit to them you've problems of your own.

A friend invites you round: she says she'd like a little natter,
says you're the one to help her on a confidential matter.
You smile, through gritted, Christian teeth and, naturally, say yes,
but how you're going to find the time is anybody's guess.
You put the blame on Paul, for saying you must run the race.
Did he not know the harm it does to go at such a pace?

You go to bed exhausted, with two minutes left to pray:
'Dear Lord, it's me: remember me? It's been too long,' you say.
'I'm not much good at listening and I'm bad at sitting still,
so you're going to have to help me, or I know I never will.
Please teach me, Lord, to lay aside the lesser things I do
and make it my priority to spend more time with you.'

Helping to pay the school fees

Laura, by this time, was at Alton Convent School. I'm sure she won't mind me saying that her entrance exam marks were rather lower than were required. However, by some fluke (we prefer to call it prayer), she was invited for an interview with the headmistress. That clinched it. Reverend Mother said she could see by Laura's bright eyes that she wasn't daft; she said she warmed to her, she would love to have her in the school and did she have any questions she would like to ask? Laura said yes, she would like to know what time they had lunch. That's my girl. Such an academic. Her first teacher, Mrs Wightman, said she wasn't a high-flier, she was probably a 'five GCSE type', but she was a lovely girl and a pleasure to have in the school. As it happened, those bright eyes saw her through school and university, emerging triumphant at the end of it all with a Batchelor of Arts degree.

To help pay the convent fees, I went back to teaching class music one day a week, at Daneshill, a private school near Reading. In the morning I gave piano lessons and in the afternoon I took the lower school classes for music. I was given a completely free rein and made the most of my opportunity to write some decent children's songs that didn't major on witches and dragons. Or fairies. Absolutely not fairies! We used to take percussion instruments outside and march round the building bashing them and singing 'What a Mighty God We serve'. Imagine that these days. Such goings-on would probably be considered offensive to other faiths (not to mention the surrounding neighbours).

I wrote a Christmas musical called *Have We Any Room For Jesus?* which resulted in a stream of Christian parents queuing up after the performance to say how delighted they were that their children were having such input, and thanking me for making it all such fun. Two of my fellow teachers were already Christians and it wasn't long before the headmistress had seen the light. They were good times.

As well as working at Daneshill, I was becoming increasingly involved with the music at Alton Convent and was more or less the school's official accompanist. I was able to compose or arrange things for them and thoroughly enjoyed it all. We once did a recording for a television programme, with Charlie on the flute (note the change of name – our younger daughter was now refusing to answer to Charlotte), Laura in the choir and me on the piano. We were doing a medley of Christmas songs that I had arranged. There was great family excitement as we sat down to watch the programme a few days later, but, since we appeared to be the only convent household with their television aerial pointing in the wrong direction, we missed it. Typical.

We also did the Morning Service for Radio Four. This involved the choir, orchestra and me on the organ and was broadcast live from the school chapel – the whole thing being directed by sound engineers in an enormous lorry outside in the car park. We never saw the men from start to finish but heard them bellowing instructions over the sound system, the most embarrassing bellow being, 'Organist, you are far too loud!' Since it was a live broadcast and the Morning Story which preceded it had overrun, the producer had to make a last-minute decision. He announced over the loudspeaker that we would be cutting a verse from the final hymn (which happened to be one of mine), and the fifth formers were so cross they threatened to walk out. I had about ten seconds to convince them I didn't mind and persuade them to stay put.

The convent's Head of Music and I were totally on the same wavelength and got on extremely well. She conducted and I accompanied, and we were a good team. Although she trusted me, she was used to the fact that I didn't always play what was written and was liable to improvise when I was bored. On one occasion, she conducted the final bar of a piece, ending with a great flourish, but I carried on with a little jazzy bit. She threw her baton in the air, folded her arms and waited until I stopped. Our audiences had become used to this kind of behaviour and lapped it up.

Every accompanist needs to have faith in their page-turner and I have mostly been given ones who could be trusted. However, when you have a great many individual pages of photo-copied music in front of you, it only takes one second's lack of concentration to land them all on the floor. I got more cheers than ever before or since on the evening of such a disaster. Somehow, I kept going and reached the final bar just before my embarrassed page-turner had managed to put everything back in the right order. You could say it serves me right for illegally copying music. You've probably already said it.

I remember doing a show on two consecutive evenings and Reverend Mother Madeleine, the headmistress, came to the first. When she also turned up on the second evening I made some comment about being a glutton for punishment and said I hoped she wouldn't be bored, hearing the same thing over again. She replied, 'On the contrary, my dear, it'll be quite different. The reason I've come again tonight is because you never play the same thing twice.'

The day after the show, I had planned to go and see my sister, Maggie, at Oxford. She was a great sister and always fun to be with, but had fought a battle with cancer for fourteen years and was now very near the end of it. When I came home that evening, Rob was standing in the drive to meet me and I could tell straight away that something had happened. Maggie's husband had just rung to say she had passed away. Another of our family had gone to glory.

This side of heaven

This side of heaven, we know just in part,
but then we shall know with all of our heart;
for what is unseen and what is unknown
will one day to trusting hearts be shown.

This side of heaven, the things he has done
are promises now of what is to come;
he's leading us onward to all that is planned
when one day in glory we shall stand.

This side of heaven we're fixing our eyes
on running the race and winning the prize;
for we have been chosen and called by his grace
and one day we'll see him face to face.

But nothing we've earned can take us there,
the truth of our faith is sure,
and only by mercy will we share
his glorious home for evermore!

Oh what a day, Oh what a day it will be!
Oh what a sight, Oh what a sight we will see!
Oh what a song, Oh what a song we will sing
when we spend eternity worshipping Jesus the King!

Decision time

On 19 October 1987, two days after 'the big storm', Rob and I were invited to dinner with some friends, Chris and Fran Oldroyd. They had also invited another couple, David and Jo Williams, with whom, they felt, we would get on really well. I'm always rather nervous when someone feels that; it's not always the case! Thankfully, we got on famously and that evening was to lead to a really special time in my musical and spiritual life.

Jo had a wonderful singing voice and was looking for an accompanist. We arranged to meet up the following week and see how we got on. The minute we 'struck up' we sensed what can only be described as an anointing of God. It was an overwhelming feeling and we just knew that we were intended to have a ministry together. It is often retrospectively that one realises the Lord's reasons for doing things. We don't always see it at the time; sometimes it takes years to fully recognise what good ideas he has. In our case, Jo and I knew immediately what we were being called to do. We rehearsed at every available opportunity and began writing our own material. We put together a programme of songs and testimony and took it to churches, small groups, large groups, village halls – whoever would have us. We produced a song book, made two albums, and for the next few years we had a full schedule, getting out there and using our gifts for God's glory. We were grateful for his grace and inspiration – grateful too for the Oldroyds' dinner party.

We always have a good laugh with Jo and David, and the day they came to Sunday lunch was no exception. David was a curate at a church in Alton and after lunch he had to nip off and take a double christening. He had been gone about half an hour when Jo's baby needed a clean nappy. The nappies were in the car. The car was at the church. The need for a nappy was an urgent one, so I drove Jo into Alton.

The service would have started by now so she would have to somehow sneak into the vestry, find the car keys, get the nappy, return the keys and sneak back out. However, the service hadn't started, two sets of christening guests were patiently waiting and David was panicking because the organist hadn't turned up. I was summoned from the car. The organ was a huge, three-manual beast of an instrument and I had never seen anything like it before, let alone played one. Now it was my turn to panic. David opened the service with profuse apologies for keeping people waiting and 'huge thanks to our organist, who only came here for a nappy'.

Our daughters, now both at the convent, were understandably wanting to go to church locally with their friends. We thought this was probably a good idea, although Rob and I still wanted to attend St Mary's. Logistically, it was a problem dropping them off at the New Frontiers church in Alton, then dashing to Basingstoke to play the organ. They spent a lot of time sitting outside on a wall, waiting for the doors to open.

We managed it for a while, then had to think and pray really seriously about what we should be doing. Apart from anything else, we felt it was important to worship as a family, in the same place. As we could see the girls had no intention of budging on the subject, we joined them at Alton. I admired my husband for even considering going, since the church was of the Free Evangelical variety and rather more free than he felt comfortable with. After a few years, I could tell Sunday was becoming Rob's least favourite day of the week, and we returned to St Mary's.

Our return coincided with the opening of their new auditorium, built to enable them to have one morning service instead of the previous two. It meant that two music groups would be amalgamating, and the group leaders were most gracious in stepping aside when it was proposed that I should oversee a new group. It was a real privilege to work for the next ten years with some very accomplished musicians, and I will always be grateful for the opportunity to serve God amongst them. We produced a style of worship which apparently became known locally as the St Mary's Sound (I was unaware of that title being bestowed upon us until quite recently), and it was good. There were a few of us in the band who liked to jazz things up and often, as people left after the service, we sent them out 'New Orleans style'. In fact, they didn't leave; most of them wouldn't move until we had finished!

Birth of *The Bridge*

My reaction to Laura's departure to university was rather unexpected. I had anticipated that I would find it hard to see her go but hadn't reckoned on crying for a fortnight. Every time someone mentioned her name I burst into tears. It wasn't even that she was miles away (she was, in fact, only at Winchester, so couldn't have been much nearer) but it just felt like the end of an era. We missed her dreadfully but were thrilled to see her doing so well (eat your heart out, Mrs Wightman) and enjoying life. I was proud of her, not least because she kept her strong faith, and didn't have a holiday from Jesus like I had done.

Boyfriends came and went but it was the pastor's son from the New Frontiers Church in Alton who turned out to be Mr Right. We liked him very much and welcomed him into our family without reservation and with great thankfulness. Mark had just graduated from Aston University and was intending to stay in Birmingham to start work as a graphic designer. They married soon after graduating and Laura got a teaching job at Wolverhampton, with responsibility for music in the school. She discovered, as I had done, that so many songs for children feature witches, ghosts, dragons and other things she didn't wish to sing about, so she asked me to write some songs and also some recorder pieces which her recorder group played in a Music Festival at Lichfield Cathedral, winning their section. This was the encouragement I needed to find myself a publisher. I took myself off to the National Exhibition Centre at Birmingham on the week of the Education Show. I wandered round hundreds of stands with my folder of recorder tunes, unable to find anyone who would take any interest. I was on the point of giving up and going home when a charming young man asked if he could help. I told him about my recorder tunes. I was aware of sounding rather pathetic and wished I could have said I had something more impressive like a two-hour musical based on the crucifixion. However, he didn't laugh at me; instead he said, 'We don't actually do recorder stuff. We are a Christian company so we do more, well . . . Christian stuff.' Had there been a feather in the vicinity, I could have been knocked down by it. 'Now, if you had worship songs in your folder, we could start talking.' They weren't in my folder; they were at home. To be honest, a Christian music company was the last thing I was looking for, so consumed was I with the desire to get my recorder tunes world famous.

My worship songs were on the desk of Kevin Mayhew Publishers within a week, and two weeks later I was invited to Suffolk for a meeting with Kevin and his marketing director, Jonathan Bugden. They asked me where my heart was with regard to worship songs; what did I really feel passionate about? I said my heartfelt concern was for the many churches that want to progress from the old but at the same time fight shy of the new, who find themselves in a gap between the two, pursuing a style of worship that misses out on the richness of either and ends up being mediocre. My passion was to write meaningful songs that bridged that gap. I was too busy congratulating myself for sounding unusually articulate to notice that Kevin's jaw had dropped, considerably.

'Do you know, Susie, just before you arrived, Jonathan and I were saying we wished we could find someone who could help us bridge the gap in worship songs – we used those very same words!'

He showed me to a room where I was brought a delicious lunch, and said they would like to go off and have a chat. I hadn't, for one minute, dared to imagine anything much would come out of my long journey to Suffolk, but it was beginning to look like it had been worth it.

Half an hour later I was invited back to Kevin's office. 'Well, we've had a talk and we'd like to ask you to compile a new song book. We just think that you're the right person to do it. How would you feel about that?' This time it was my jaw that dropped. How did I feel? I felt they were putting an awful lot of trust in someone they'd only just met, that's how I felt. I opened my mouth to give him an answer but was lost for words. 'Right', said Kevin, 'we need to come up with a title.'

In 2001, after eighteen months of very hard work, *The Bridge* songbook was finally published. Born out of a desire to cross the denominational, doctrinal and musical divide between churches, it contained four hundred and twenty-seven songs, twenty-five of which were mine, and I had the privilege of choosing them all. I trawled through hundreds of hymns, songs and recordings, aware of the huge responsibility I had been given to produce a resource that would be imaginative, theologically sound and meaningful. It was a mammoth task and I loved it. Having written many hymn tunes himself, my father had taken a great interest in the project and I was especially glad that *The Bridge* was published in time for him to share the excitement before he died, aged ninety-five, a year later.

Charlie, by this time, had graduated from Southampton University, was living back at home and working locally as a physiotherapist. It was always a great relief to us that both our daughters knew what they wanted to do career-wise, got on and did it, and did it well. We are proud of them.

Charlie is a fairly private person and it was frustratingly difficult to extract any information out of her with regard to boyfriends. However, there came a time when the radiance on her beautiful face rather gave the game away, and so it was that we were introduced to the man responsible for putting it there. A few months later, he asked for her hand in marriage, saying, 'You've made me so welcome in your family, I'd like to stay please!' Both our sons-in-law are called Mark (which can get confusing), both are musical, and both are great men of faith. We thank God for them.

Soon after Laura had been Charlie and Mark's 'bridesmaid with the bump', she produced our first grandchild, Naomi Grace. We discovered that being grandparents was the greatest privilege, the biggest joy and the best thing ever.

Rob had begun his own tennis court company in 1989 and as well as compiling *The Bridge*, I was his office manager. We had converted a large double garage and I worked from home, whilst Rob went out and about. I'm not too good at relaxing and much prefer to keep busy, so I quite enjoyed the challenge of two different types of employment, run concurrently from the same desk. Composition is something that requires inspiration; you have to capture an idea as soon as it comes into your head and write it down before it disappears. Oh, the frustration of a customer ringing about their tennis court just when an idea had come into my head! Many a tune has been irretrievably lost on account of someone's moss problems.

When we were first married, Rob promised that one day, when he could afford it, he would buy me a grand piano. It had always been my dream but I couldn't see it becoming a reality. However, true to his word (albeit thirty-one years later), he bought me a beautiful French grand. When we first went to look at it, we discovered that its owner, as well as playing the piano, played the violin. In order to try out the piano I suggested to the woman that we had 'a bit of a jam' together. She picked up her fiddle and I could tell immediately from her confident poise that she was going to be good. I remember thinking, 'I bet she didn't learn her instrument in a cupboard with four other people and an irate teacher.' She put some music in front of me and, without my glasses, I couldn't see how many sharps there were, but there were quite a few. I struggled through, badly. She sailed through, beautifully. In fact, she was so good, she could have been a professional. When I got home I put her name in Google and discovered that she was. In fact, she was described as being 'one of Britain's leading female violinists'. And I had suggested a bit of a jam . . .

I was now writing more and more and even took my manuscript book to bed with me, finding that creativity was often greater in the early hours when I couldn't sleep. Poor Rob used to mumble into his pillow that he pitied Beethoven's wife. When I pointed out that Beethoven wasn't married, Rob grunted, 'Well, I'm not surprised.'

Three books of children's songs, a jazz Eucharist, jazz arrangements of traditional hymns and five musicals followed. Having wished I could have told the young man at the Education Show that I had a full-scale musical on the crucifixion, by 2004 I had written one. It took three months to write the whole thing and, knowing that Andrew Lloyd Webber doesn't write his own lyrics, I allowed myself a degree of smug satisfaction.

Alive! To Tell The Story was put on at Basingstoke's Haymarket Theatre and involved some seventy cast members, plus a small orchestra in the pit. It was very moving and well received but it was not without its stressful moments, and by the end of it I was exhausted.

Throughout the rehearsals and performances of *Alive!* I had endured a frozen shoulder, making playing (and conducting at the same time) jolly painful. After nearly nine months of physiotherapy there was no real improvement and I noticed that my left hand was now being uncooperative and my hands and feet tingled, especially when I was trying to get to sleep. I had no energy and seemed to have less enthusiasm for things, which wasn't like me. I also realised that when I sat next to someone, in church for instance, my left arm would jerk and dig them in the ribs. This was definitely not normal behaviour and clearly something was up . . .

Parkinson's: mine for life

On Thursday, 24 March 2005, I sat with my friend Ruth in the waiting room of St Peter's Hospital, Chertsey. My left arm was doing its usual thing, and merrily digging her in the ribs. Rob wasn't able to be there, but, so that we could find out what was going on as soon as possible, had paid for me to see a neurologist privately – any minute now, in fact.

It was seven o clock in the evening and, since he was clearly wanting to get home to his supper, this man was not going to bother with pleasantries, and I was launched straight into various neurological tests. He wanted to watch me go down the corridor to see if my left arm swung when I walked. It didn't. He asked me to close my eyes and then touch my nose. I couldn't. He asked if I had a tremor. I hadn't. After many more tests he sat at his desk, picked up a pencil and twiddled it under his nose as one would twiddle a handlebar moustache. He carried on twiddling and asked me which I would like first, the good news or the bad. Being a bit of a coward I opted for the good. 'Okay, the good news is you probably won't die of it.' I said that was nice and prepared myself for what was coming next. 'The bad news', he announced, 'is that you have Parkinson's disease,' adding, without even drawing breath, 'Look it up on the official Parkinson's website; don't read any old rubbish. Any questions?' I would have questioned who on earth let him into the medical profession, had I been brave enough. Instead, I found myself being remarkably, strangely calm.

I asked how it was likely to progress; he said there was no way of telling because everyone was different. I asked if it was hereditary; he said there was no evidence to say whether it was or it wasn't. In short, he didn't really have the answers, so I stopped asking the questions. I had just received the most shattering news of my life and wanted to get home to my husband. He had just received nearly a hundred pounds for delivering said news and wanted to get home to his supper.

Ruth drove me home and for much of the journey I sat in stunned silence. It was slowly dawning on me that life would never be the same again. I had Parkinson's, there was no cure and I would have it for the rest of my days. It wasn't an illness that I would get better from; it was a condition that would only get worse. I suddenly felt very alone and more than a little scared.

I hadn't for one minute considered the possibility of having the disease, even though my Aunt Mary had battled with it for twenty-five years. I had always found her rather frightening, partly because of the immobility of her face, which meant that she rarely smiled. She shuffled when she walked, spoke quietly through tight lips, and had the most incredibly small writing you ever saw. Did I have all that to come? I remembered the neurologist saying that everyone was different and I hoped I would be very different from Aunt Mary.

As we neared home, I wondered how I should put the news to my husband. I was aware that it was going to affect his future as much as mine. Having grown up with a disabled mother, Rob was used to having to be a carer, but it didn't seem fair that he was now lumbered with me as well. He didn't use words, but just gave me the longest, strongest hug ever. That said it all: we were going to face this thing together.

One of the hymns that mother used to sing around the house went like this:

Yes, this is the God we adore,
our faithful, unchangeable friend,
whose love is as great as his power
and knows neither measure nor end.
'Tis Jesus, the first and the last

whose spirit shall guide us safe home;
we'll praise him for all that is past
and trust him for all that's to come.

I could almost hear her singing it now. We would be trusting God for all that was to come, that was for sure.

The next day was Good Friday; the whole family was to be together and I was determined that it should indeed be a good Friday and not a bad one. It has always been a fascination to us that Rob and I could have produced two children so completely different in their nature and personality from the same recipe, so to speak. Laura is very outgoing, with an infectious enthusiasm for life – the kind of person who lights up the room on entering it. To be in her company is wonderful, if not a little exhausting! You can rely on her to get things done (but mention the word 'bossy' and she will tell you she prefers the term 'graciously organising', because, 'let's face it Mother, someone has to be'). The rest of us are not great decision-makers and are thankful to have someone in the family who is.

Daughter number two is quite different. There is a quiet serenity about Charlie which brings a calming presence whenever she is around. It is an attribute which I greatly value and rather envy. Her consistent temperament and lovely nature have won her much respect and many friends. How blessed we are to have such a varied combination of super qualities in our children!

It was no surprise, therefore, to see their contrasting reactions to my news. Laura immediately burst into tears; Charlie walked calmly to the kitchen and returned with a box of tissues.

I wanted them to be reassured that I was still quite normal and said that the most helpful thing they could do would be to treat me as such. I wasn't intending to make a big deal out of it and I didn't want them to either. Laura asked lots of questions; Charlie said very little, but the next day sent me the most lovely letter, in which she said: 'Although it's all a little worrying, we also need to see it as exciting as it draws us closer to God and makes us dependent on him. I've been thinking about why God allows particular illnesses for particular people. I guess if he wants to get a message across to a pianist, he doesn't home in on their feet! Obviously, we have no say in the matter but it does determine what we learn from it and how God uses the situation. He is clearly wanting you to sit up and take notice of him and I'm looking forward to seeing what he is going to do in your life in the coming years!' I couldn't have asked for more positive encouragement, and, especially coming from my own daughter, it meant so much.

I live, dependent on Jesus

I live, dependent on Jesus, in everything I do,
being sure that he who has promised
is faithful, good and true.
Being confident I'm forgiven
and stains of guilt are gone,
I live, secure in his keeping,
as my Saviour leads me on.

I live, dependent on Jesus, in everything I do,
being sure, when trouble surrounds me,
his love surrounds me too.
Being confident of his guidance
wherever I may be,
my feet are firm on the pathway
as my Saviour walks with me.

I live, dependent on Jesus in everything I do,
being sure that he will sustain me
in all he takes me through.
For Jesus is the solid rock
I build my life upon
and, by the power of his Spirit,
in my weakness I am strong.

For I can do all things
in him who strengthens me.
In the power of Jesus, King of kings,
is where my strength shall be.

My house has never been arrayed with so many pot plants and flowers as in the days following my diagnosis. I was overwhelmed by the love and concern of friends; in fact, I felt a bit of a fraud because I felt completely well and had no visible signs of being anything other than normal.

Without wishing to sound ungrateful, there were just a few people whose words of encouragement were best consumed with a pinch of salt! One friend came to see me and confidently announced that the Lord was going to heal me of Parkinson's in November. Since it was then April, despite my lack of mathematical talent, I was able to calculate that I would only have seven months to put up with it. I saw my friend again in November and, as nothing had happened, she said she thought it might be more towards the end of November. The following January I pointed out that November had been and gone and she said she wasn't sure what year the Lord had meant! Another friend told me of the advances in treatment, cheerily adding, 'It's wonderful - they can even drill a hole right through your skull!' Thankfully, I was given the grace to not be troubled by the misplaced words of those who meant well!

A few weeks after seeing the neurologist, I had an appointment for an MRI brain scan. This was to rule out any other possible causes of my symptoms and (according to my cheeky son-in-law) to check that I did, indeed, have a brain. The pencil-twiddler had given me his mobile number and I was to ring it to get the results. He said I could ring him any time I liked, so I did. 'Ah, yes,' he said, 'I'm actually up a ladder painting my daughter's bedroom at this precise moment, but I'm sure we'd have heard if anything was amiss.' Unbelievable!

He's on my case

I initially elected not to go on any medication. It was all part of the denial process: if I wasn't treating the Parkinson's it was easier to pretend I didn't have it. I know people who spend every waking moment investigating all they can about the disease, attending lectures on it, going on special diets for it, in an all-consuming battle which rules their life. That's their choice, of course. Rightly or wrongly, I made the decision from day one that my life would rule the battle, not the other way round. And nearly eleven years on, I think I'm doing pretty well. (It is, of course, not me doing pretty well, but God who is doing pretty well in me. To him be the glory!)

People sometimes ask if was cross with God when I was diagnosed with Parkinson's. I wasn't so much cross as mystified. Mystified that, having served him with my hands for thirty years, he should allow me to have a condition that affected them – and I told him as much. His reply was mind-blowing: 'It wasn't your hands I wanted; it was your heart.' I was completely stunned. Music was my life, a gift which I had always believed was from God – and now he was saying it wasn't what he was after. He wasn't making a great deal of sense!

Slowly, very slowly, I came to realise what God meant. It wasn't that he hadn't given me the gift, it wasn't that he hadn't anointed me to play, it wasn't that he wasn't using me: it was that my focus had been on my hands instead of my Lord. I had somehow felt that was sufficient: as long as I composed meaningful songs, as long as I played in the kind of way that helped people to worship, then I was doing what the Lord required of me. I'm not making excuses, but it can get quite busy at the piano when you are leading worship. You worry about whether you have made the right choice of songs (because that's a responsibility in itself). You worry about your music being in the right order (it was when you left home but has a habit of mysteriously reshuffling itself in your music folder). You hope that everyone in the band will remember the repeats (but it will be you who forgets them). You spend the sermon thinking of what to play during Communion (because you'd forgotten it was the third Sunday in the month). In short, you are so preoccupied with practicalities, the chances of actually imbibing some spiritual benefit are not great.

My role as Music Director was now in question: I was finding playing tiring and difficult, I was having lapses of concentration and, more to the point, I felt my heart wasn't in it. To come to terms with all that after a lifetime of playing standing on my head (which I did once) was so hard. I didn't want to let anyone down but I knew I was unlikely to be able to cope now. I made the vicar aware of the situation and said I would try and carry on until we found a successor. Within a month, someone came up to me and said he was new to the church, he was a pianist, and if ever we needed one he would like to get involved. Hallelujah!

Not for the first time, Rob and I were faced with a decision on where we should now worship. We felt it would be sensible and less tiring to go to church locally, bearing in mind that I was likely to get worse someday. I also wondered how I would cope with seeing the music group every Sunday and not being part of it. With considerable mixed feelings, we left, again.

We went back to Harvest Church at Alton and within three weeks I had an email: they couldn't find a keyboard player (notice free church term for pianist) for the following Sunday and could I please step in. Now I was totally confused! I was under the impression that the Almighty was wanting me to step down, not in. I decided he must have a good reason for allowing this request, so I agreed to play just once. Thankfully, I rarely tremor, except when I'm very cold or nervous. Since, on that

Sunday, I was the latter, I prayed really hard that I wouldn't have to endure the embarrassment of being shaky. It is customary in free churches for prayers, words of knowledge or prophecies to come 'from the floor' without warning. Occasionally, some brave soul will start up a song and the keyboard player, if able to establish what key they are in, might join in. This takes some courage. About ten minutes into the service, a voice from the back began to sing, 'He is my fortress, I will never be shaken . . .' Never be shaken! Would you believe it! I joined in with a grin on my face, a confidence in my fingers and an assurance in my heart that God knew my fears.

Having waited so long for the promised grand piano, it was now being neglected. This was partly because I couldn't seem to persuade my left hand to do anything sensible and partly because I was depressed and uninspired. After two years, I reluctantly conceded that medication was necessary and thus began a lifetime's daily regime of shovelling chemicals down my throat. It confirmed what I suspected: that the scientists of today can put men on the moon, but are unable to manufacture a little pill without side effects.

Many people had kindly prayed for my healing and I had come to two conclusions on the subject. The first was concerning services where one is invited to 'Come on down!' It takes some people a lot of courage to leave their seat and join the huddles down the front: I am one of them. When I didn't have the confidence to venture down the aisle, it left me feeling guilty, awkward and, yes, un-prayed for. Jesus said to the blind man, 'What do you want me to do for you?' when it must have been blindingly obvious (sorry, couldn't resist). That does suggest that he likes us to ask, that making a public stand is important to him. However, I wasn't convinced that he refuses healing to those who are up the back or along the side. If he was going to heal me, he would heal me where I was. The second conclusion

I came to was this: despite the crowds who drive miles to see the 'big names' with a healing ministry, if it is in the name of Jesus, the biggest name of all, that we are healed, why waste the petrol?

Having come to those conclusions, I surprised myself by agreeing to go to a healing service in a small church in Tichfield. I was invited by a dear friend, Sue, who had cancer of the spleen. The service was very low-key and the visiting speaker was an unassuming, smiley evangelist from Brazil. He wasn't a big name; in fact, I can't remember his name at all.

He delivered his talk, with many apologies for his poor English, and then asked God whom he should pray for. He said there was someone there with a problem in the spleen area. 'That'll be me!' said Sue and hopped out the front, grinning madly. The church was so small she didn't have far to hop. Next he asked if there was someone with a brain tumour and a twelve-year-old girl went forward. He called forward ten people in all and prayed for them. No mention was made of anyone with Parkinson's so I stayed put. That was fine. The dear lady at the piano hadn't quite grasped the concept of playing quietly in the background during a time of ministry. It was deafening. I was sitting just inches away from the loudspeaker and was sorely tempted to turn her down a bit.

After the service, people went through to the church lounge to have coffee and Rob and I and Sue and her husband were just about to follow, when the Brazilian came over to us. He said he had been watching me and would I like him to pray for me. I am quite hard of hearing and it suddenly dawned on me that I wouldn't have heard a thing with that lady on her piano. God hadn't forgotten me – he was just waiting until she'd gone for coffee! Yes, I'd love to be prayed for, please!

Within seconds I was lying on the floor. Now, I want to make it very clear that this was something I was never, ever going to let happen. As very new Christians we had been on a house party and, after one meeting, people were going down like flies. There were five doctors on the house party, none of whom was making any attempt to check these poor people over. I feared we were all in for some kind of holiday virus. But no, it was apparently a condition know as 'slain in the Spirit', highly contagious in charismatic circles, the recommended treatment for which was just to go with the flow and get plenty of rest (by the looks of it, on the floor).

That was it: I resolved to never have anything to do with such attention-seeking, drama queen stuff. It was not my scene, and, anyway, people had told me you get pushed. No wonder some folk had Christians marked down as an odd bunch. It was that kind of behaviour that confirmed it.

However, I am neither odd nor attention-seeking, I am no drama queen, I hadn't been pushed, and – albeit through a glorious haze – I heard the man praying for things he couldn't possibly have known about unless God had told him. He was no big name, just a humble chap whom God used to remind me who's boss.

When I get fearful or despondent, I think back to that evening and the comfort it brought me to be reminded that the Name above all names is in charge, he knows all about me and he's on my case.

Don't forget we're C of E

Knowing how much hard-earned money Rob had paid for it, I was feeling guilty about my piano. My limited ability made me so cross and frustrated that I preferred not to play it at all. I was utterly depressed. A friend said that I should count my blessings and look on the bright side (was there one?) because some people had never played the piano in the first place. She meant well, but I felt like poking her eyes out! Without music I didn't feel like me. In fact, on a bad day, I felt completely useless.

I was aware that an increase in medication might make a difference but was equally aware of the side effects. My lovely Parkinson's nurse specialist completely understood my reluctance, and came up with a suggestion. This was the deal: she would write me a prescription for more drugs and I could redeem it now, this year, next year, whenever I felt I was ready. Within a month I had got them.

A few months later, something of great significance happened: Rob and I were given tickets to go and hear Alfred Brendel at Basingstoke's Anvil Theatre – a world-famous pianist and one of my favourites. At the end of the concert, in response to the audience's demands for an encore, he played a Schubert impromptu. As he played, I realised that the left hand didn't have a lot to do. I also remembered that I used to play the piece in my teens. When I got home I searched through my music; it was faded and falling to pieces but it was there. With some trepidation I sat at the piano, for the first time in months, and began. It wasn't good, my hands were stiff, but it was a start, and to my amazement, I discovered I was now able to play semi-quavers (they're the busy ones). I played it and played it until I knew it off by heart and have played it almost every day since. The corner had been turned.

Although we were now going to Harvest Church in Alton, we still popped back occasionally to St Mary's at Basingstoke. We had so many friends there and we missed them. I had a sneaking feeling that we wouldn't stay at Harvest Church. One day one of our friends at St Mary's came right out with it: 'Look, you Hares, you know jolly well you'll end up back here so for goodness sake get on with it!'

Our indecision regarding where we should go to church was getting us a bit of a reputation. We had left St Mary's the first time in order to keep the family worshipping together, and, for the second time, to make my life easier. Although we felt at the time that they were justifiable reasons, we weren't really happy. Now we were hopping from one to the other, which was unsettling; we weren't committed to either and we knew we must make another decision and, this time, stick to it!

Don't forget we're C of E

Well, here I am in church today,
I stand to sing and sit to pray.
The pastor does his preach, and then
I give him seven out of ten.

The music group is pretty dire;
my husband would prefer a choir
in robes resplendent, singing stuff
that has some depth. He's had enough.

His eyes are closing, not in prayer,
but much more likely in despair.
A voice shouts, 'Praise the Lord!' and then
another cries, 'Amen! Amen!'

They're lost in wonder, love and praise
and I just stand here in a daze.
Why is it that I get so bored
here in the presence of the Lord?

I'm sure the fault's entirely mine,
the folk around me all seem fine.
Why is it that I can't engage?
The words flow onto every page
of songs I write, so unrestrained,
yet here I stand, unmoved, contained.

Perhaps I should put on an act
(I'm sure some people do in fact)
but God would rather I was real
— at least, I hope that's how he'd feel.

There's no point in denying it,
this isn't home, we just don't fit.
Lord, put us where we're meant to be
(and don't forget we're C of E).

We returned to St Mary's, fearing that we might now be viewed as a couple of spiritual boomerangs. We needn't have worried; we were welcomed back with open arms and much love. I don't believe our little foray into the free church had been a mistake; we experienced a lot and God taught us a lot. I think we concluded that different denominations provide for our spiritual food just as different supermarkets provide for our bodily food. We may have a preference as to where we get our sustenance – whether for our body or our soul – but the important thing is finding a menu that suits our particular digestive system and making sure we eat!

One of the things that excited me about coming 'back home' was that I was immediately invited to join a prayer triplet. I knew that such groups were great things to get involved in, but had always shied away from being committed to one. More fool me! These times of fellowship are now a part of my life that I couldn't be without. It is a real privilege to be able to support and encourage one another and Denise, Jane and Katrina are very treasured friends. (You will have noted that there are four in our triplet. This is because we don't want to be split up, not because we can't count.)

Another thing for which I am really grateful is the willingness of those responsible for choosing songs to very kindly (and quite often) choose mine. Although I'd had that period when I didn't touch the piano, I had never stopped writing, and Gill, Roger and Ed – in whose hands the music now was – were very gracious in receiving my contributions to the church repertoire.

Out of the darkness

Out of the darkness of the night
Jesus called me.
Into the radiance of his light
Jesus brought me,
giving my life a brand-new start,
changing my cold and stubborn heart.
Now I am his adopted child,
rescued, ransomed, reconciled!

Wonderful, glorious day!
Jesus saved me,
washing my sins all away.
He will keep changing and
changing me till that day,
when in heaven I stand,
perfect in him.
O wonderful, glorious day!

Out of a life of guilt and sin
Jesus called me.
Into a life that honours him
Jesus brought me,
choosing this sinner for his own,
making this humble heart his home.
Now I am his, I'm justified –
purchased, pardoned, purified!

No greater sacrifice was made:
Jesus made it.
No greater debt was ever paid:
Jesus paid it.
No greater love, no greater grace;
bearing the cross, he took my place.
Now I'm forgiven, now I'm free,
all because he died for me.

The writing of worship songs is a huge responsibility. One is putting words into people's mouths which must be theologically sound and grammatically correct, tunes into people's heads which are melodic and memorable, and inspiration into people's hearts which will bring them closer to God. I have learnt all that now, but my initial song writing as a new Christian had involved opening the Bible, shutting my eyes and stabbing my finger at a verse. If I didn't like the look of it I re-shut my eyes and repeated the process until I found one I did like. It was hardly the right way to go about it.

After my diagnosis, something new began to happen. I found that God was anointing me to write songs with greater depth and more meaningful words than ever before. They were so filling my head, I could hardly cope with them all! It wasn't unusual to have to stop my car in a lay-by and scribble a tune down before I forgot it. Songs were now coming out of life's experience and it was humbling to be the recipient of such grace outpoured.

I thought back to what my work colleague had said about God not always stopping things but always using them. I thought back to what Charlie had said in her letter about looking forward to seeing what God was going to do in my life in the coming years. I thought back to what God had said about wanting my heart, not my hands. I put all three of them together and they made perfect sense: the reason God didn't stop my Parkinson's was because he knew it would change and shape my future. He knew if my heart was in the right place, the focus would be on him and he would get the glory. I should have known he'd have it all planned.

There are many curious things about this disease, not least its unpredictable nature, which means that planning ahead is difficult. You never quite know when your body will decide to have a day off and be uncooperative. Once I was struggling to get dressed and having finally claimed victory over the doing up of buttons, I decided to move a wardrobe. This I achieved, on my own, with no trouble at all. Strange.

When you're diagnosed with Parkinson's you almost have to draw a line under life, revisit everything you were, did and thought and start again. Not many things can remain as they were before; that was life then, this is life now. Such a drastic reshuffle affects everything. Many people's concept of the disease is that it's basically a physical thing. They see the tremors, the shuffling, the rigidity, the slowness: but what they don't see are the fears, the lack of confidence, the guilt of being a burden, the pain that keeps you awake at night – and much, much more.

Having said that, despite all the difficulties and frustrations that Parkinson's has introduced into my life, over the years they have become the norm for me and made me who I now am. If, by some miracle, I suddenly didn't have the disease, I would probably feel even more odd!

They call me Gritty Granny

Rob and I realise how blessed we are to have daughters, sons-in-law and grandchildren who all get on so well and who all love each other. We live in an age when close families are, sadly, not that common. Included in our family is Fi, a young widow, who came into our lives several years ago and whom we think of as a kind of adopted daughter. She fits into our mad bunch well and is a great blessing to us. The traditional, annual family holiday is something we all look forward to and Rob and I are touched that everyone is still happy to come away with the oldies. Would it have something to do with who foots the bill, perhaps?

Our grandchildren, Naomi, Jacob, Rhys, Owen and Jed, are, of course, the best in the whole world and are our greatest joy. My concern has always been that I will become a shaky old dodderer who can no longer kick a football with the boys in the garden: that I will develop a staring, unsmiling 'moon face' – typical of Parkinson's – and they will think I'm a miserable old trout. However, their obvious love for me has cast such fears to one side. The younger ones accept me as I am because they have never known me be anything else. I have a rather special relationship with fourteen-year-old Naomi and am very touched by her fundraising efforts for Parkinson's, her constant encouragement, and especially her faithful prayers. She and Jacob have witnessed the changes in me and are more likely to remark on them. A few years ago I overheard them having this conversation:

Jacob: 'Why is Granny slow at doing things?'

Naomi: 'You know we're not supposed to talk about Granny like that.'

Jacob: 'But she is though.'

Naomi: 'It's because of her Parkinson's disease and you don't know anything about Parkinson's Jacob so don't talk about her again.'

Jacob: 'I do know about it.'

Naomi: 'So what is it then?'

Jacob: 'It's something to do with when you can't park a car.'

This Parkinson's lark

Whenever this jolly disease gets me down
and life seems a bit of a trial,
I think back to something my grandson said
and it always makes me smile.

According to Jacob, then six and a half
(just shows how astute children are),
this Parkinson's lark is an illness you get
when you're rubbish at parking a car.

My heart, not my hands

There is one person without whom I could not be and whose dedication to making my life easier is remarkable. The man who married me for better or for worse, in sickness and in health, to love and to cherish, has more than lived up to his vows. Rob hasn't seen Parkinson's as just my problem; we are in this together, adapting together and learning together. It's not just my life that hasn't gone quite as expected; it's his as well. We have always been a good team, and never more so than now. We share tasks in the kitchen (I make the mess, he clears it up) and it has recently come to light that my husband has a passion for ironing. Interesting that he hasn't mentioned that in forty-three years of marriage. He says it gives him a great sense of satisfaction, and who am I to deny him that.

I have a wonderful husband, I am surrounded by a terrific family and many supportive, encouraging, praying friends. That's what I call blessing.

My consultant tells me I am doing well. I am fortunate to still be driving, still playing my beloved piano, still playing badminton once a week and still looking relatively normal. The latter (I'm sure my cheeky son-in-law would say) is, of course, a matter of opinion.

There are many, many people with my condition whose battle is much greater and whose stories are far more worthy of telling. I am humbled that God should have called me to share my ramblings, which would seem rather insignificant if compared to theirs.

I am aware of what the words 'progressive disease' imply and realise that someday my battle may intensify. There is no knowing.

Does God plan for us to be ill, is suffering some kind of punishment? These are questions which many people the world over are asking. To answer them in the affirmative would conflict with our experience of a loving, caring God. It is a complete mystery why some people face such challenges, whilst others seem to sail through life with barely a scratch.

In Scripture we read that in all things God works for the good of those who love him, in order that they might be conformed to the likeness of his Son. We can, therefore, be sure that when we go through difficulties and hardships, God, in his love and mercy, will use our situation to make us more like Jesus.

Do I sometimes question why I have Parkinson's? Of course I do, but the reality is that I have been changed because of it, and God's grace has now enabled me to live a different song.

Who has planned the journey?

Who has planned the journey for life that lies ahead?
Who has made the pathway for every step I tread?
Who has seen a future that no one else can see?
Only the Creator of all that I will be.

Who can give the reasons for all that's in the past?
Who can give the answers to questions not yet asked?
Who can keep in safety the days ordained for me?
Only the Creator of all that I will be.

Who will give life's picture its colours and design?
Who will make the sorrows and joys to intertwine?
Who will weave the pattern designed in secrecy?
Only the Creator of all that I will be.

This is my Creator, my times are in his hands;
I will walk the pathway, surrendered to his plans.
He will walk beside me until this life is done,
he who made and loves me, my Lord,
the faithful one.

Greater are the plans of him who sees it all,
who knows my heart, who holds my days.
His thoughts are not my thoughts,
his ways are not my ways.
Greater, much greater are his plans.

Lyrics to Songs

Who has planned the journey?

(CD Track 1)

Who has planned the journey for life that lies ahead?
Who has made the pathway for every step I tread?
Who has seen a future that no one else can see?
Only the Creator of all that I will be.

Greater are the plans of him who sees it all,
who knows my heart, who holds my days.
His thoughts are not my thoughts, his ways are not my ways.
Greater, much greater are his plans.

Who can give the reasons for all that's in the past?
Who can know the answers to questions not yet asked?
Who can keep, in safety, the days ordained for me?
Only the Creator of all that I will be.

Refrain

Who will give life's picture its colours and design?
Who will make the sorrows and joys to intertwine?
Who will weave the pattern designed in secrecy?
Only the Creator of all that I will be.

Refrain

This is my Creator, my times are in his hands;
I will walk the pathway surrendered to his plans.
He will walk beside me until this life is done,
he who made and loves me, my Lord, the faithful one.

Refrain twice to end

I stand on a rock

(CD Track 2)

I stand on a rock that is secure, that won't be shaken,
for you are a faithful God.
I stand on a promise that is sure, that won't be broken,
for you are a faithful God.
You're my refuge, strong deliverer, great are the things you've done.
You're the mighty, all-sustaining, all-sufficient one.

Yesterday, today, for ever,
you can be relied upon.
You will always be my treasure,
this will always be my song.

I walk on a path that is made straight by you before me,
for you are a faithful God.
I walk in a power that keeps firm my feet beneath me,
for you are a faithful God.
You're my guardian, never sleeping, watching me night and day.
You're unchanging, you're unfailing, good in every way.

Refrain

I live by a grace that set me free from condemnation,
for you are a faithful God.
I live by a love that won for me a free salvation,
for you a faithful God.
You're the joy that lifts my sadness,
faithful in all you do.
You're the strength that fills my weakness,
I depend on you.

Refrain twice to end

No greater love

(CD Track 3)

No greater love was ever known,
nor such compassion ever shown,
than on the cross of Calvary
where Jesus gave his life for me.
Amazing love, amazing grace:
Jesus my Redeemer dying in my place.
    The Sinless King, the Righteous One:
gift from God the Father
    of his one and only Son.

No greater sacrifice was made,
nor such a ransom ever paid,
than when the spotless Lamb stood in
to pay the price for all my sin.
Amazing love that saw my shame,
giving me forgiveness, taking all the blame,
    that I, the guilty one, could be
washed and cleansed for ever
    by the blood he shed for me.

No greater pain was ever borne,
nor such a crowd so full of scorn,
as with their shouts of 'Crucify!'
they stood and watched the Saviour die.
Amazing love that took my sins
to the cross of Jesus, nailed them there with him.
    The Son of God, in agony,
crying to the Father:
    'Why have you forsaken me?'

This King of kings who came to save
went from the cross into the grave,
but death could never keep him in
and from the grave he rose again.
Amazing love that won for me
hope of life eternal bought at Calvary.
　The risen King, who reigns above,
died to be my Saviour;
　　there could be no greater love.

Amazing love that won for me
hope of life eternal bought at Calvary.
　The risen King, who reigns above,
died to be my Saviour;
　　there could be no greater love.

From the heights of glory
(CD Track 4)

From the heights of glory, to a humble birth,
the Lord of heaven came down to earth.
And the greatest story of salvation's plan,
in a stable room began.

What a gift, what a gift we are given;
sacrifice of the Father for us.
What a gift, what a gift we are given;
King of kings, Lord of lords, Jesus!

From a humble stable, to a world of shame,
the friend of sinners, who calls my name
with a heart of mercy,
brought the love of heav'n,
and it gave lives hope again.

Refrain

From a life, so perfect, to a cruel cross,
the world's redemption, the Father's loss;
and the nails were driven and the blood flowed free
in the hands outstretched for me.

Refrain

From the grave he's risen, ever glorified,
to take his place at his Father's side;
and the greatest glory will be ours to own
when he comes to take us home.

Refrain

What a hope, what a hope we are given;
sacrifice of the Father for us.
What a song, to proclaim 'He is risen!'
King of kings, Lord of lords, Jesus!
King of kings, Lord of lords,

Out of the darkness

(CD Track 5)

Out of the darkness of the night
    Jesus called me.
Into the radiance of his light
    Jesus brought me,
giving my life a brand-new start,
changing my cold and stubborn heart.
Now I am his adopted child,
    rescued, ransomed, reconciled!

Wonderful, glorious day!
    Jesus saved me,
washing my sins all away.
He will keep changing and changing me
till that day, when in heaven I stand,
    perfect in him.
O wonderful, glorious day!

Out of a life of guilt and sin
    Jesus called me.
Into a life that honours him
    Jesus brought me,
choosing this sinner for his own,
making this humble heart his home.
Now I am his, I'm justified –
    purchased, pardoned, purified!

Refrain

No greater sacrifice was made:
    Jesus made it.
No greater debt was ever paid:
    Jesus paid it.
No greater love, no greater grace;
bearing the cross, he took my place.
Now I'm forgiven, now I'm free,
    all because he died for me.

Refrain twice

O wonderful, glorious day!

Look out for 2 new CDs
of Susie Hare songs,
plus 2 full-music books
that feature all the
songs on the CDs.

For more information,
please visit our website:

www.kevinmayhew.com